M000237925

BLACK HOLE FACTORY

BLACK HOLE
FACTORY

POEMS

Eric Smith

UNIVERSITY OF TAMPA PRESS

Copyright © 2018 by Eric Smith. All rights reserved.

Manufactured in the United States of America
Printed on acid-free paper ∞
First Edition

On the Cover:
Julie Heffernan, "Self-Portrait as Great Acceleration," oil on canvas, 67 x 60 inches.
Copyright © 2016 by Julie Heffernan. All rights reserved.
Reproduced by permission of the artist.

Cover design by Joshua Steward

No part of this book may be reproduced, stored in a retrieval system, or transmitted in any form or by any means, electronic, mechanical, photocopying, recording, or otherwise, except as may be expressly permitted by the applicable copyright statutes or in writing by the publisher.

The University of Tampa Press
401 West Kennedy Boulevard
Tampa, FL 33606

ISBN 978-159732-161-7(pbk.)
ISBN 978-159732-162-4 (hbk.)

Browse & order online at
http://utpress.ut.edu

Library of Congress Cataloging-in-Publication Data

Names: Smith, J. Eric (James Eric), 1982- author.
Title: Black hole factory : poems / Eric Smith.
Description: First edition. | Tampa, FL : University of Tampa Press, [2018] |
  Includes bibliographical references.
Identifiers: LCCN 2018031793| ISBN 9781597321617 (pbk : alk. paper) | ISBN
  9781597321624 (hbk : alk. paper)
Classification: LCC PS3619.M588225 A6 2018 | DDC 811/.6--dc23
LC record available at: https://lccn.loc.gov/2018031793

Contents

For Laura

I.

A Show of Hands

They hang there, just inside out
of reach, pressed into service
by sleeves and yawns, able to bear
in their bowl the answer to thirst.

No surprise the first maps traced
four hills knuckling the horizon,
the palm's indiscriminate furrows
bisecting fields of loss and love.

As children, we learned from them
the truth of faith and architecture:
here's the church, here's the steeple,
open the door—

Even before we knew this sanctuary,
the walls of caves were gloved
in the narrative of hands, and history
lay stunned beneath their applause.

Powerless nights still summon the pair
to resist the thunder's clap.
Beneath a rain-battered roof, they coax
from shadow a menagerie of beasts:

A crocodile emerges to snatch a hare.
Swans raise their necks' quiet questions.
A butterfly cracks a chrysalis of fists
to flutter over the threadbare dark.

Tyrannosaurus Sex

In the loose silt of a riverbed, unlatched from gravity
tethering them to earth, they overcome
their weight to fall into something
that, in its thumbless grope, resembles
the adolescence of desire.

Ice Ages are forgotten, as is what's left
of the night, emptied of its mammalian chatter.
Their bodies are less than welcome
to themselves, much less one another,
each bleat of pleasure met with a jagged wound.

New theories about sex, much like the old,
are guesswork. But who can say if lovemaking
for them was ineffectual, the vacancy of coupling
an invention of the Pleistocene?

Monogamous as shirt sleeves,
they huddle against meteoric rains
that end with fire. What if the violence
of their bodies is the reason the sky has room
for stars? Nature aches for symmetry

found in another. Here, in the widening pool
of night, the moon is tied to its mirror
in the water, and the stars, blazing out
of holes punched in the black canopy,
scatter the first light on the first night's love.

Cryptozoology

I can never know you as I know speech,
the dappled murmur of its river.
But I yearn for proof of you, missing link,
ellipse in evolution's unfinished sentence:
You, Sasquatch. You, Bigfoot. You, Yeti,
scavenging the syntax of dreams. Abominable,

the tongue to the mouth, unable
to muscle through the brambles of speech.
You rhyme with nothing. And yet,
pressed into the forgetful clay of this river,
the way a pair of O's ghosts a sentence,
is an echo of your knees, when you knelt to drink

from the murk of your reflection. Unsure, I blink
away the cobwebs veiling fact from fable.
You are the subject of our human sentence,
or part of it, near the headwaters of speech.
A switchback in history, wandering like a river.
In it, our names for you branch: Wendigo, Yeti,

Honey Island Swamp Monster. Yet I
worry that if we forge the link
between us, the mystery of you lies riven,
the myth unraveling like a cable.
I'd rather you span subcontinents of speech
and lurk, ancestral antecedent, in the sentence

of our origin. Or better, be that sentence
unfinished, a plot point we have not yet
locked up in our own mouth's speech.
Clanking against the hull of night, be a link
in the trawler's anchor chain, a sibyl-
ant syllable, a shadow scrying the river

on the far side of sleep. Or be the river,
insubordinate to the ocean's sentences,
exclamations of rain. They are erasable
as all things are. Or should be. For you, Yeti,
I leave this void, this gap, this _____.
Fill it with anything but speech.

Song

Who sings to stones abandoned by the tides,
these rituals of sand? The names we offer god

are all that's left, like untranslated scripture.
The day's last gull snags its reflection in a slur

of water. We were told of a belief required of us
without reason. We were told there would be

confusing rains. The hour unravels as it must.
And what comes after: sunset, a smear of rust.

And what comes after sunset? A smear of rust,
confusing rains. The hour unravels as it must

without reason. We were told there would be
water. We were told of a belief required of us.

The day's last gull snags its reflection in a slur
of all that's left, like untranslated scripture:

these rituals of sand. The names we offer god
who sings to stones abandoned by the tides.

Sandhill Crane

A wineskin sloshing on stilts, you decant
a nauseous honk. Your eyes are beads of honey,
gray feathers watered down in weak coffee.
Why cock your scarlet head? What you want

rarely emerges from frost, and no worm
wriggles in this upturned earth. Straight-legged,
you wait, watch morning unshell from its egg.
Hive-minded drone of this weathered swarm,

what you excavate is yours—speckled frog,
serpent's cursive S. Ground allows you these
dissections, frantic aerator beak-deep
in black loam. Soon, ghost, swath of living fog,

this will green and you'll be gone. Forgive
the prairie's subtlety—like nothing else alive.

Tricolored Heron

Pale weathervane, you wear the sky's patchwork—
an overcast grumble of cloud on your chest.
Along your neck, a ribbon of earth's rust
stains your blue needle stitching cloud to murk.

Waters you wade are mirrors. All fish you fish
are mirrors. The lidless eye, the unblinking
that waits above the lily's eaves. You slink
among the reeds, waiting for chirr or splash

to dent the air, and then you blur—
thrice-fletched arrow fast in the fast heart
of your prey. A struggle, succumbing to art

like this: you pin it down in mud until
the marsh returns to its hush. Waters still.
On them, the shadow you are or never were.

Marrow

What I want from want is only its hunger.

Not the story it tells of fire
to fire. Not the brass nocturnes it sings
to the cilantro bolting in cracked clay.
Not the pale cereus suckling the moon's bright filaments.

What I want from want is a silence
pilfered from a burned-down house,
the last syllable of its collapse into ash. I want
its origin, the city at the heart of its country
of desire, where every inch of sidewalk is thirsty for rain.

An inwardness offered those who have diagrammed the syntax
of sheets. Who enter an argument as wind enters a church.
The nave is high enough to forge its own weather.
Hymns unfold like maps with all the seas erased.

Not the lightning's yellow bones, but its marrow.

All I want is to admit that what I wanted, all this time, was not want
at all, but you, and the way you answer the question
of loss, which both of us know as a silence
that opens and shuts and opens
between the stuttering hinges of the paper moth's wings.

Orrery

That summer or spring, before or after the shuttle bloomed,
we learned that a body in flight worships only velocity.

Having forgotten the equation that solved for God,
everything we felt then was scripted in a room

missing one wall. The stars burned like tiny televisions.
After the credits, we watched as the sky, black as bruises,

lost its narrative arc. We terraformed the backwaters
of syndication, and sawed the hours in half

to free them of improvisation. Fate threaded its contrail
to the pale altar at which we, trembling, lay our trembling,

and we fed our children to the reruns of a dream.
In their rest there was an innocence, sheared

from sleep, soothing as the bulb tonguing the socket.
Such stars we catapulted to the heavens in bright thousands

to colonize the night, rocketing against all that nothing
with only the promise of mid-season renewal. To see

heroes pinned to the body's outlines eventually erased
by rain was to see, in the cruiser light that stained us

with caution and concern, that ours was the witness,
ours the laughter in its can. The sun was a white tablet

fizzing in dusk's glass. The sky's menagerie grew restless.
And when the satellite fell from the nadir of its aging

blazon, we trained all the glass eyes starved of light
on bodies in slow arcs at the outer edge of their ardor,

on the horizon where the last of the light succumbed
to static, and everyone got what was coming to them

in the finale, tomorrow or next year or never
which will, far faster than we ever imagined, arrive.

II.

Story Problems

Let's start with two trains
  clattering out of two stations
    nearly two thousand miles apart,
miraculously
on time, twinned steel skins
  winking in early light
    beneath two skies textbook
in their cloudy- and blue-ness.

The trains' passengers
  and related baggage are equal
    in number. Their respective conductors
are of similar weight
and jocularity.
  Assume wind speed, elevation
    and the demands of
small children remain constant.

Train A sheds the platform's
  nervous buzz, the waving hankies
    of tearful grandmas,
then angles southward.
B will head north, leaving
  behind a gaggle of
    stewards in white gloves
bored and anachronistic.

Let's say I'm on A.
  Rust red tracks mumble through the unkempt
    hills dotted with herds
of single-wide trailers.

You're on B, arrowing
through the quilted countryside.
    Shorebirds have followed you.
The sun tills the horizon.

But before day dies,
    too tired for any more puzzles,
        take what we know. Let's work this out
hypothetically.
Given distance, time,
    and where we want to be,
        in which one-horse whistle stop
does the story end? Let's say

you've been given me,
    the ever-variable x—
        ex-boy, ex-toy, execrable
break-up mixtape maker.
On the equal sign's
    far side, I wait, clutching
        what remains of us now sundered,
the solution approaching its null.

Or roughly halfway
    we look up as our trains pull out,
        leaving from some Podunk Nowhere,
and happen to catch
glimpses of each other
    on separate trains,
        our angles of coincidence
equaling the sum of longing.

Or there's an accident.
   A lineman got his signals crossed
and flipped the track switcher too soon.
News crews eat it up.
One train plus one train
   equals one train. Today
      equals one burning
field, my hand plus or minus yours.

Reading the Classics

Grown tired of every euphemism
    for genitals,
summer camp embellishments
       fading faster than a farmer's tan,
the arguments over how one spells
    the body's emissions (*is it cum or jizz or jism?*),

you retreated to the susurrus
    of central air,
to camp out in the dusty stacks
       with peeling labels, among the Classics and Romantics,
who (so it seemed) knew desire
    was an equation of longing adding up to more than coitus.

You traced the hidden metonyms
    in pots of basil,
counted the rows that lined the gardens
       of sonnets, sounded out declensions of ardor
Ovid knew, and unpacked puns
    on country matters, to place your tongue inside an idiom

you felt in breath's iambic stammer.
    Through epochs of hex-
ameter, you learned your art—
       scrawny, asthmatic Vulcan, your pen a hammer—
scribbling in the notebook's spiral heart.
    Even then you knew; poetry is never as good as sex,

young penitent before the altar
    of halter tops
and cut-offs. Inapproachable as naiads,

your beloveds displayed the severed heads
they'd clipped from *Spin* and *Bop*—
   so like the busts of ancient heroes—on the doors of their lockers.

But then, a miracle. You got a date
   with Suzy Chapman.
It seemed impossible. She was a junior.
      You were, well, you—your voice still prone to fracture.
You couldn't imagine how this could happen,
   sure all week that Atropos would scissor the thread of fate.

That Friday night, you said a prayer
   to Clearasil
and every god of adolescence,
      and convinced innocence and inexperience
were both *hamartia* and Achilles heel,
   anointed yourself (too much) with your father's Drakkar Noir.

Desperate to be liked, you tried
   an antic disposition,
affected Keats's consumptive cough.
      Being yourself would never be enough.
You needed Coleridge meets Cobain,
   heard *Lasciate ogni speranza, voi ch'intrate*, considered suicide.

The top of your head was safe.
   But you chickened
out, didn't even call her. You dunce.
      You'd smithereened your only chance
with her, Baucis to your Philemon.
   You dreaded Monday. The stares. The note in your locker: *WTF?*

Instead, you fell asleep over the *Aeneid,*
    watched *Monstervision*
on TNT. The VCR
      blinked its digital ode to the midnight hour.
You dreamed: the oak embraced the linden.
    In their branches, a silver light. A skylark's passable aubade.

A Lot

At once a vacancy, a plenitude;
   a square of brindled earth rubbed bare by wind;
     a chit on which you've scratched your name or mark;

     a forest razed for cars; a narrative arc,
   minus of course the minor desecration
of its initial plosive. Of creation, one could say, *dude,*

that's like, a lot.
   In the beginning, there was of light and dark a lot
     of each, and some guy huffing on the sea,

     then handed one's lot in life—to be the wife of a lot
   of Lots—you wedded a future in funerary
gray. Fed your salts, foretelling flames dream

for you the rest: wheat stalks or whittled bones cast
   inside the day inside the night inside his fist.

D & J Quality Plumbing

White as vertebrae, hollow as birds,
I filled a cardboard box with fittings:
the Ys, Ls, and Ts of water's vowelless

alphabet. I dragged into crawlspaces
succumbing to cricket and cobweb,
addressed the ruptures we repaired.

A house is a body. Pale pipe branches
beneath the joists from sink to toilet,
and drains descend to darkness, bear

pressures that scald and soothe. Your hands,
stigmatic with violet blotches of primer.
The acetylene coughing to life in its bottle.

Hanging pipe was just a way to maintain
a ledger: eighty bucks an opening,
plus material. Enough for what we need,

but not what we owe. No matter the house,
the wall studs haunted by snarls of wire,
there were two rules: Shit rolls downhill.

Payday's Friday. Yet others, half-heard,
gurgle in homes asleep inside themselves,
unable to dislodge the bolus of grief.

What we are is shaped not by light, but thirst,
everything in us that remains unquenched
mapping the square footage of childhood

disappointments. Like this one, which earns
less than what you'd bill for setting out
a single sink. For you I leave a quarter inch

of fall, a bubble off-level to ensure gravity's
departures. And as I shed my caul of sweat,
and let the water unstitch the day's knots,

in the swipe of a hand across a mirror fogged
with steam, I see this face that has begun,
in your reflection, to see itself.

Melon

I had heard the legend: a boy who stole
one from a neighbor, then knifed a hole
in it, held it until he spilled his seed
inside. At summer's end, he pried

it open, swore he saw in the ruddy flesh
a pair of eyes blink at him, tiny fists
reaching desperately for a father's touch—
a son of sorts, this redneck homunculus.

I nurtured a kind of florid reverence
for the lie, its fecund, weeviled truth,
even if it was nothing like the elegance
my grandmother coaxed out of the earth.

Her favorite was Moon and Stars.
After dinner, she'd snip one off the vine,
let it chill through supper in her Frigidaire,
then slice herself a smile of blushing rind.

I always refused. Not even a bite.
Its stars reminded me of my own freckles,
and the queasy blotch of its yellow satellite—
too soft to touch, like an infant's fontanelle.

The Shed

Through the unhinged door, the cycloptic eye
of his old Ford squints through its lid of rust,
pries open the moth-chewed dark, and fixes us
with its gaze. For a moment, I am paralyzed:

he had knelt to show me how to work a rasp,
explained that backward strokes will ruin the edge.
But the past isn't what I'm here to salvage,
though it feels that way. Above me, paper wasps

have hung their gray lantern. From a metal cage,
a bulb sloughs its light. On his workbench,
ghosts haunt the pegboard, every file and wrench,
the hand saws, teeth brittle and softened with age.

He'd outlined them all with a black Magic Marker,
to remember the proper place for each.
So much reminds, remains of him. I touch
the un-sunned wood inside the lines, far darker.

In a Cool, Dry Place

Not where coffee waits for the percolator's
tortured weeping. Not inside the spent shells
of orange bottles, shedding prescription labels
like moth wings. Not near the radiator's

phthisic cough, past the silk-hinged doors
of spiders, or beneath these window sills
warped by epochs of sleet. Not among the kills,
cocooned against lack, hunger's strung idolaters.

Not in the cedar chest beneath the yellowed veil.
Not in the brittle envelope's twice-stamped tomb.
Not anywhere I might think to look for blame,

a map, an answer—anything that could reveal
this cool, dry place in which my parents cradle the name
for everything that went wrong between them.

Homecoming

My father hated it. And worse, the washed-out stars
burning the local headlines, who went as far
as graduation, then to work—grinding out hours
on their heels, rerunning dropped passes, sour
dip spit in their frowns. Today, pro-grade turf
hides scabs of sod on which we flipped-off curfew,
kicking empties through the uprights. My friends
are boosters now, and fathers: model citizens
who swapped the scoreboard's bulbs for LEDs.
My name never graced its sad, blinking vacancy.
Distance, my painter friend says, creates an illusion
of perspective. Beyond the ads for Verizon
wasn't him, but me, back after years away.
I scanned crumbling stands for the face of a boy
who bayed at other boys, a stitch of shadow
that I once was: a self I barely recognized, but knew
as much as I know him, like football and fall.
As anyone knows one's father. Hardly at all.

Picking Muscadines on Ray Mountain Road

This is not an origin story. But once, a seed slipped
into a fist of earth, and made from this hunger another.

The vine turned at the sun's reproach, and blushed.
And in culverts quieted by quilts of early fog,

the leaves greened and murmured as light swelled.
Maybe you descended the steppe of history

like an accident of conquest, a footnote in the narrative
of the razed. Maybe you were the sugar that shaded

the altar on which wisdom first rang its brass bell.
Who can say? When I reach for the tart glissando

of your sweet beating, I think not of silences,
but of the knife that sang its lullaby to the whetstone,

and the light that laddered the ditch, a reminder
that each of us keeps time with some other heart.

There will be an ending, as there always is
for the body. But for a moment, let there be

only these hands, this knife, this boy—
pockets filled, about to burst, with you.

Questions Concerning Galactic Bowling

The palm-fanned pharaohs of ancient Egypt
should have reasons for wanting pyramids
of slender pins or gourds lined up along
the Nile's wide banks by pinchasers

who, by their sweat- and sun-lashed backs,
probably have other names for this game.
For me, alone in this constellation
of tables and feet we pay too much for,

I don't know what else to call it. A past
in which time's window passes one frame
after another. A parade of shutters reset
by the twisting hydraulics of pin-setter

machines. The DayGlo parrots are out there
piping, and as I watch their voices flutter
out over the lanes, I wonder how long
we will struggle against the bondage of laces

and eyelets, the ill-fit of shoes we pay
to return? The phone on the wall jangles
with questions about fourteen-pound balls
and whether or not we can walk with them,

and I wonder when these people, chained
to these racks loaded with neon ballast,
will ever abandon this ship, or will we
simply stay aboard as it runs aground

on a sandbar that mirrors our denial?
Bad music even our parents forgot
urges us on to the careful rhythm of a Dutch
two-hundred, unwilling to offer the glory

of a game more perfect, afraid of a body's
mistakes, and while the salt on our lips
is not the delta's freedom, let us find solace
in the quiet maze of belts returning balls

to their proper racks. We'll dry our hands
on the lift's lazy fan, and help one another
from the gutters, and tomorrow,
pick up the pins, and try again.

Vertigo

1.

There are nights when I refuse touch,
seek refuge in something not tethered

to flesh, sure that even your murmur
of concern will crack the dull white

hammers in my head. I wait for silence
to become palpable, for a line cast

into the murk of my disease, both of us
freighting the unspoken in the cups

of our hands, waiting for the world
to untangle its wind. Say I make it

tonight without a snag, and tomorrow
hauls itself upright, its terrors lost

in transit. How even then to explain
to you, who trusts secrets to the dark

whorl of my ear, that I am broken.
What you place in me is irretrievable.

How do I say that most nights the words
unlatch from the book's page and slide

into a darkness that unstitches the spine,
that each day begins with me clinging

to the tossed deck of this unmade bed,
expecting to be swallowed by its covers?

2.

The birds are buttoned to branches,
the early notes of their throats keyed

to the wind. The sun settles in
and trees prop up that early light.

Superior slaps the ore dock's pylons.
A few gulls patrol the lower harbor,

summer clutter of sails long departed,
the boat slips surrendered to ice.

But on the horizon a hole appears
in my sight: it sucks the lake dry,

dismantles the ore dock girder
by girder. Birdsong is snipped

from air, and the birds broken
from their perches. It pries up all

the earth, flings it into that null,
dull zero leaving no stone unturned.

There is no stone. Only me, curled
around nausea, lying in this quiet:

a gray without depth, a nothing.

3.

A storm's center is called a calm.
I lean on the crutch of fact, sort

the pieces of an edge-worn puzzle
again, *ad nauseam*, as the rain arrives,

a squall blown inland that undresses
the water oaks. The wind paces

outside my apartment, batters
the stormproof panes with its fists.

I've lived in Florida a year now
and lost count of the afternoons

lashed by lightning, how often
I've watched the ceiling, crazed

with cracks, spin, and the handfuls
of pills I've swallowed to nail it

into place. The rain's static lets up
long enough to ease open a door

on the world where the cochlea,
that blind snail, drowns.

4.

The waves' dull roar crests the break
wall of Superior, a lake I am an ocean

away from now. Some nights, I listen
so hard for its crush that I ache

from the effort. I lie next to you
as black wings beat against

my sight, and everything—
bed and table, body and book—

picks up the tremble. I remember
how those first nights of winter

felt. The two of us hiked to a peak
the locals called Top of the World.

We were lost in goggles and gloves,
and our voices died in the clouds

spilling from our mouths. A storm
circled the valley. The wind blew

out of it, met the other wind snaking
between the pines, and I was held fast

in their squabble. The first flakes
spun down on silver wires.

Limbs tied knots in the night's velvet.
When the waves snapped the sheets

of ice drawn over Superior's banks,
and March had sculpted the shoreline

into moonscape, it was quiet enough
to hear the groan of the world

resisting its turning, an audible ransom
held up to that nothing on the other side

of the wind. Rocked by its lull,
I lay in that merciful quiet still.

III.

Of a Feather

*Port Authority workers have been authorized to use shotguns
to shoot down any snowy owls that may cross into the airport's airspace. . .*

Say you're on the tarmac, tenth in line
to leave LaGuardia, which (admit it) sucks.
Descending on a wing of static, the captain

mumbles monotone instructions for the stewardess.
She smiles and preps the cabin for gravity's fist.
Her eyes say this is coach, not business,

so stow your crap. You do. The runway blinks on.
It's then you notice the guy who waves the planes
is packing heat—a tactical bleeping shotgun.

You sweat like Shatner in *The Twilight Zone*,
but then recall what happened next (straitjacket,
plus an ambulance), and rather than make a scene,

you pop a Xanax, hope the beverage cart
might risk a pre-flight round. No such luck.
The plane ascends. You snooze, you land (an art,

how we avoid the vectors of disaster),
and brave the snarl of baggage claim.
You hear it in the mouth of the newscaster:

helpless airport crews were authorized
to double-barrel arm themselves and shoot to kill
these white (well, white-ish) terrors of the skies.

Picture them aloft, in an ouroboric loop.
Life, of course, is terminal, not liminal.
From where you stand, does this resemble hope?

Once home, you see a blackened seismic ridge
of mountains laced with snow, a wobbly sun—
a fantasy your kid has fastened to the fridge—

and for a moment, everything is light.
Above the peaks, in a purple marker's magic,
a storm of Vs—a child's idea of flight.

Black Hole Factory

In Switzerland, seventeen miles
of tunnels tense their ironclad sleeves,
and generators, strung-out like Christmas,
flicker on. Fiber optic bouquets bloom
along the floor as a blue-white beam, wrestled
from a star's heart, hurtles towards its twin.
Behind a window tempered like a welder's mask
you watch the world's largest particle
accelerator spin its horseless carousel,
and you hope for a continuum tear
to unlatch from the pressure of space and rattle
like a tooth in the mouth of the world.
Every second, a black hole climbs out
of dead stars collapsing under their own
mass. A stray one could devour the planet.
Poof, just like that. A shrinking ring
of blue fire chuffed out like a circle
of candles. This is a risk you understand
and repeat if only to smash the parts together,
sort through the debris, the helium halos
from the sun lying in yellow tatters.
You expected this: the dinner jacket
of the universe turned inside out
for the sake of seeing the lining,
as if those feverish origins of matter
mattered. A possibility exists
for it to chew through the narrow
prison of physics and slip, unseen, into
the green world. A week may pass before
it gobbles up the last few continents,
the mirage the survivors keep in front of them,
until their whimpers are replaced
by an absence in the equation of time:
just you, and me, and a black hole
of almost zero size orbiting the sun.

Everyday Italian with Giada De Laurentiis

Crouton is the diminutive of crust,
for which I apologize. I'm a bachelor,
simple in my tastes for red meat
and etymology. You wouldn't know the beet
is my favorite root vegetable, ludicrous
as it sounds. How could you? Spatula

in hand, you waltz across the tiles, spatula
conducting frilly collars of pie crust
to set, ready to accept the ludicrous
dollops of filling, manna to any bachelor.
Escaping the egg white's fate, you are unbeat-
able, and tender to all cuts of meat.

Forget all this preparation. Let's meet.
I want to see you in your apron, your spatula,
and nothing else. Is that too forward? I bet
I've made you uncomfortable. Please crust
me. I know you're a fan of puns, a bachelor
who knows his way around a kitchen's ludicrous

gadgets. I'll be your Fry Daddy, ludicrous
with my wide mouth and overused oil. Meet
me with breaded thighs and I'll bring a bachelor
standby: not Chianti, but Canola. Forget the spatula.
We'll stick to surfaces, our smiles the crust,
half-eaten in the sky, the moon becomes. It beats

sitting at home this weekend, cutting beets
into coins and "making them rain," as Ludacris
suggests we do. You may be a little upper-crust
for his Hotlanta shenanigans. Want to meet
me in the 706 instead? We'll take the spatula
off its rack, catch reruns of *The Bachelor*

on ABC. Listen: I tire of being the bachelor
that I'm not. I'm a man with needs, my beets
shriveling in the crisper, lonely as a spatula
in an empty drawer. I know this is ludicrous,
that what I feel is worse for me than red meat.
I keen for your no-knead bread's buttery crust.

I admit that this heart's ardor is ludicrous.
Please. Beat mine to death with your spatula.
Set fire to my bachelor pad. And of me, eat.

Mid-Century Miami

1. Pete Desjardins and Partner Dive off the High Board at the Deauville Hotel

Like a wood stork holding its bill
open as the salt air quizzes its nares,
the diving board at the Deauville,
on stilts at the water's edge, glares

at the sun. Like a spinner bait, it blinks
at the men frogging along the bottom
who gush to the surface. The light slinks
behind a chorus line of palms.

Though there's a frond-tousling wind,
a contrail blooming on the blank slate
of the sky, the pool lies flat as if filled
with stacks of chipped black plates

instead of water scoured by chlorine.
The sun, squinting gray-eyed over dunes,
robes itself in cloud. Everything's on leave.
Even the songbirds out of tune.

Unthreaded from its hypothetical screws,
two men forgive gravity's tug, and soar
into the charcoaled sky. But flight is old news,
like fire, the wheel. You ache to be with her,

propped in a lounge chair, sipping a cocktail
the color of Windex, a fresh lime wedge
floating on its surface like a main sail
with the wind knocked out of it, its edge

occasionally lipped by a coppery wind.
It rattles the fronds and putters out
over water. She relishes oblivion.
As if the sun weren't fueled by doubt.

2. *The Fontainebleu Hotel, Main Lobby*

In the silent procession of all things
mouthless, the columns in the lobby,
each bearing a plastic acanthus, ringed
with ferns and latan palms repotted

in this air-conditioned paradise, appear
like ruins thrust from the loam of a jungle
barely tamed by sparkling chandeliers.
Vines slither under couches in a tangle.

The tiles, tooth-white and cinched like bowties,
ignore the tendrils. Shined to mirrors,
they don't seem worse for wear, and why
should they? She's gone. No one here

descending the stairs, no one gowned in scales
of sapphire, no one to enter a city bristling
with the clatter of carts, alive in a mural
along the far wall. In it, a man, whistling

tunelessly, leads a horse with a load
of lumber or block into the city's center.
Or is he leaving? Facades sag into the road,
scaffolds ladder the sky as it splinters.

Candles burn down to nubs in the eyes
of empty houses. Streets, robed in rust,
swallow songs the birds discard as they fly
into that smolder in the mouth of dusk.

Millefoglie

– Postignano, Umbria

How many languages are in the human heart?
That night, we ate *millefoglie*, paper-thin

zucchini, cemented with besciamella, a recipe
inherited from refugees. Everything lingers here:

A fresco, shattered by earthquakes, reveals another fresco.
When I asked, you said it meant *a thousand leaves*.

¡Revolución!

Even the exhortations of the faithful come armed
between Sol and La Latina.
I flinch as my new tongue stampedes
out of the rings of their mouths
flanked by exclamation points sharp as picadors.
I manage a toddler's disregard
for grammar and good sense—
su perro es muy hermoso, for he is, I swear;
lo siento, I'm sorry, for being American, for being here
long after the shutters have rolled down,
putting every storefront to bed,
and darkness has muzzled the cartoon balloons of graffiti.
Through a porthole
I watch three men watch
morning rifle its light over a soccer pitch.
Even here a man will get up earlier than God to see God
winging across the midfield line.
Back home, the measure of a man
can be taken by the height of his lawn's crewcut.
We like our politicians well-armed
and our love stories to spoon with Sandra Bullock.
We die curled up around the sharp petals
of chest pain, or slough off diabetically, the body's own ellipse.

On Sunday, the anarchists gather
around the planters teeming with a nervous green,
near the tacit, stony visage of Tirso de Molina,
exchanging pamphlets and tracts photocopied
and recopied on the backs
of the Saturday-night-specials menus
stolen from restaurants where most of them are cooks.
Our new friend will only teach me words
for a woman's body. He says to me, *Don't worry.*
It's only a library. There's nothing very interesting inside.
I want to tell him back home we remain cloistered

in the ritual praise of being ordinary,
and that when December stunned the neighborhood
an impossible blue, though we had always known the word
for snow, there it was, abundant and radiant as milk,
and we escaped into the darkness and drifts of its unfamiliar
fricatives, in a world stripped of its echo,
among trees locked in prisons of ice.

Three Hundred Byzantine Horse Skulls

Who among us can say *osteoarcheology*
without it colonizing the jaw's soft loam?
Odd, to describe its pre-Hellenic roots
as *Byzantine*, tripping down the unicursal
corridor etched elaborately in the throat.
There is something dark within it.
It squats in the horned depths, bridled
by the burden of the past, gathering the dust
of centuries, on the river's far shore
that recent history names the Bosphorus.
Descend the tunnel of its riparian etymology
and emerge at *a path or strait for cattle*,
under which are found all of these skulls
dreaming beneath the senility of the sea.
And beneath them are still the bones
of ships, awaiting our excavation.

I think of you, my friend, with a fistful of salt.
You've sewn its savor shut in a bag of *throumbes*,
those olives free of all blemish, obese with oil,
that will wait for you a year or more, under
the pressure of bricks, drinking of the dark
brine, unraveling its secret. It is a luxury
to return to our beginning, to shed that in us
still animal, ruminant, which aches for the earth
and what it offers. For you, I have lit this votive.
It sits in the cradle of one of the horse's skulls.
I let the smoke write on it, darkening at the fault
lines between bones. This place where we meet,
origin and union, beneath flesh and hide
and the syllables of dust, where it is easier
to imagine that we can remain unchanged.

IV.

Step Well

The rain is a boy with empty pockets
lurking in the elder, eyeing the leaves'
greening vanes. This boy, the rain,
glistening beneath the cricket's trill,
empties a cistern into the mud he makes
of our origins. The sky tears open.
In full retreat and speechless, the moon,
that jug of hollers, doesn't care,
and ladles the light into his mouth.
As the rain straddles the horizon,
a wall of cloud cottons the sky.
The water spilled, he cleaves.
When he says nothing, we listen:
little tongues clambering between
the leaves. Now we're the ones fit
to leave gaps in ourselves to catch
the rain. We remember that only
the brightest points are water-tight.
And the boy rains quietly in the rain.

The Arsonist's Lament

If like fire I could lash the fields
and climb the crowns of pines
to test the air with my tongue,

could I rewrite the dark
codices in the library of flame?
Or would I bed down in the horn

of a ram, quiet as the moth's
applause? I hymn the wires
in the walls of an empty room

that once ached with light. I burn
like those who spell the hidden names
of kerosene on yellow grasses.

I have watched the world emerge
from a ductile seed, have seen men
raise their sons in fists of smoke

and stamp on the sky dark alphabets
full of syllables so raw they sting
the throat. I lift myself to that song.

Tent Worms (in the Shade of the Pecan Tree)

And the limb-wreckers
pitched their sticky, sun-bleached tents,
gnawed the leaves to lace, made sieves
of them for light and the blue-fringed air.
I raised a ladder to the clerestories
of leaves, mouthed my prayers
to the gods with little red teeth,
and in a ratchet of sparks, coughed
the torch to life. I kindled the nests,
set fire to sleep—a violence I knew
as intimately as the seasons' change.
I pried open one pale tangle,
found in it the mute warmth of hands
into which I dared not press my own.
I worried that when carried back
into light, whatever lay hidden in that silk
wasn't meant for me. I dreamed
in groves, the trunks' black smudges
repeating, where I ate of myself
beyond satiation. If anything might hold
some softness, some secret freight—
a gray seed locked in the fist
of all cotton; a bead of rain, frozen
and black as a crow's eye—let it come.
Let the hammers of summer bend me
to the earth. Under the chewed eaves
let me be soothed to sleep
by the rustle of leaves. I have waited
here for you to pack my dreams
with gossamer. For your mouths
to sew me into silence.
For your hands, blackened with worry,
to hold out the heart of all fire,
setting me loose to writhe inside its heat.

Sky Valley Rider

Slipping among abandoned pines, a fox
noses the air. Smoke, that semaphore
of urgent burning, columnar and pale
against the blue-black bruise of night,
obscures the flicker of far-off fire.
A hot wind mutters through a skull.

Even stripped, what is there this skull
can't see? Its emptiness eyes the fox
loping across the kindled field like fire
unraveling, those flames a semaphore
of memory in this owl-haunted night,
fingernail moon newly waned and pale.

What the dead wouldn't give for the pale
red of ember, a tongue's return to the skull
to utter, even if only to fill the night,
its senseless chatter. For the fox,
what was grass or brush is semaphore,
inscrutable shadow now slashed by fire.

Perhaps they're scriptures, scrawled by fire
on a field left dryer than paper, pale
and undisturbed. If so, wind's semaphore,
a whistle low and toothless as a skull,
becomes its most holy vowel. The fox
is a frail clutch of yelps. Night is night.

Or night is a mirror in which night
reflects the sky's mute turning, and fire
shatters it into song. Listen for the fox,
its needling laughter stitching pale
notes to the chorus inside the skull—
warning no one hears, a semaphore

unheeded by ships of cloud. Semaphores
of starlight guide them across night.
Lithe fingers of grass caress the skull.
The grass, in turn, is consumed by fire.
What remains—nocturnal, defiant, pale
flicker barking against darkness—is the fox,

no semaphore. In the skull,
there is only night, where even the fox
is nothing: pale reminder of a dying fire.

Hortensia

On this shore, am I
so near the satin heart
of the sea that it over-
hears the oars shearing
the tin hues of salt? Or
is the sea now tarnished
like the heron's throat?
To its anthers: hither,
hornets. I am to her
as rain, a riot of ash.
There is no hero
in the heart's arson.
Staggering ashore now,
I hear only this
thrashing of the stars.

Field Guide

If the earth has yielded to the unchanging
seasons, and you have coaxed the shadows
down out of the trees, you may then admit
that the body, raw, naked and singed, is a river.

You will be powerless to dull its quickening.
But if the night, ill with beasts, begins to leave
snarls of itself laced to wire the men in your past
have strung between furrows, then wait for the moon

to lower its pale horns before you invoke the stillness
found only in the fire's hymn to smoke.
In doing so, you will see the brittle patina
appear among the leaves. From this, fashion

a cloak for a season you have not yet named.
And remember: loss is a gift the body receives
like bread. And if it is your father who emerges
from the worm-gnawed dark, let the crows

settle their own accounts. Draw for him a bowl
of milk to rub into the sore knots. For you are
the storm—keep the bluest sparks in your mouth.
Supplicant, yield. Wet-nurse the constellations

scattered in the unplowed sky, those wanderers
in the perpetual guttering of what it might mean
to be, in this rude clamor of light, a daughter
wearing, as if she was meant to, a brother's skin.

ICU

Tide out today, and the shore remains
unfinished. Gulls fish the cryptic
silences of stone, hungry for the mussels'

black hinges clinging there. Lavender
sweetens the memory of distant fields.
The inland hills are freckled with sheep.

As shadows unravel beneath the bare
knuckles of the linden, I let myself forget
how you lifted the brittle infinities

of the nautilus to your ear, heard it whisper
not the name of the sea, but of a fire
sharpening driftwood into dark points

aimed at the lidded lights of the stars.
When its heat had surrendered to ash,
you said, *I will make of myself a mansion*

to loss, and polish its windows with a rag
of song folded, so carefully, in my pocket.
This was the rock heavy enough to ballast

the bone-white hull of the moon.
You, laughing on its milk-scrubbed decks.
Left to me: a pair of combs whittled

from the bleached pelvis of a ewe.
A handful of nails wrapped in the leaves
of a hyacinth. I think of you, an oracle

of salt. I understand why no one ever asks
the evening tide for surcease or censure.
For clemency, this is how I beg the sky.

Stele: Corinth Baptist Church Cemetery

You preferred the white flowers of the potter's field,
the leaves' creased prows spinning in the gutter,
the black gate as it clicked shut behind the rain.

One night, after the night laid down its hands,
you held out like a secret a bowl full of stars.
I offered you the white flowers of the potter's field.

What were you listening for inside that hour
you wound and held so close to your ear?
The black gate clicking shut behind the rain?

When you reached for me in the tangled dark,
I fell apart like an aspirin in a glass of water,
dreaming of white flowers in the potter's field.

As the hearse probed the shush of traffic,
umbrellas collapsed in the quiet, like prayer.
The black gate clicked shut behind the rain.

Tonight, again, the moon is a cradle of scar.
What will happen to us is no nearer, no farther.
The black gate opens on the potter's field.
The white flowers click shut behind the rain.

Toward Morning

There were women here
    once, squatting on the shore,
casting knots of bread
    into the spillway for bream,
coaxing chubsucker and bullhead
    from their torpor.
I waited for the thunder's report,

    for the wake's white italics
scrawled by the reckless fist
    of the water's heart,
for the splinter of frost
    in my blood to thaw.
The sky bent to its mirror.
    I skipped a stone,

watched the crease that mars
    the water's skin
until it faded. The moon
    dulled the lake
from bronze to tin.
    I counted the scars,
watched them sink into the murk.

    At the edge of the slough,
a stillness—frogs in the reeds,
    cypress roots clutching a skein
of fog—and in it, I understood
    what I would mean,
eventually, to you.
    Never enough.

The Mercy Dancers

i.m. Michael Shane Smith

How could I tell you that I listened to your last breath enter
the room, that it banged the shutters of illness that left you

drenched in a rented bed in a paper gown. I was two rooms
and as many decades away. I was trying to find a memory

with a bit of sun in it. Maybe one with your window down,
palm hammering out the songs of summer you saw recede

in the rearview. How could I tell you that the moon splintered
into nine choirs as your mother unlaced the knot of her hands

from the bedrail. By leaving, she left you room enough to leave
the ruin of your body. You had spared her this departure,

which for both of you, though it's difficult to say so, was a mercy.

*

mercy of frost   rummaging the pockets   of bruise-blue firs
mercy of wind   whistling in black sockets   of the antlered dead
mercy the steps of a man   who wasn't winter   but knew its name

mercy for all   who humble themselves   before loss
mercy   only mercy   for the moments
we forever inter   in these inadequate graves

*

Headlights lanced the wen of silence embedded in the night.
We leaned against the peeling slats of your porch, drinking beer

and watching stars unravel above Cashtown. Around us, the air
was a green dance of fireflies. The black insistence of the crickets

accompanied them. As I left that night, a shadow shadowing
the pines between us, you shouted something, but my memory

is large enough to admit only the shape of your voice,
not what it held. I wish now for the small mercy

that would allow me to open the envelope of night,
to reveal what it was you had written

on the last hour of the last time I saw you.

*

mercy of the maple   in october   abscission
mercy of her singer   asleep beneath   its cowl
mercy of the last cough   of butane   in a cheap lighter

mercy for the steadiness   it offers the hand   of the smoker
mercy of the dew   lingering   in a hoofprint
in the family plot   off corinth road   mercy for the lilies

lined up on her hearth   the pale ellipse of their petals

*

Call them the mercy dancers, those moments of hesitation
in which some part of us performs, unasked, an act of contrition.

Call them the answer, riddling the dark, beyond the baffling
enterprise of human being. Call them the arcs we draw between

the stars to clarify, if only for a moment, the celestial narrative
of which we are but a glimmer. Call them what braces

for the hurricane of a loved one's anger when the winds are behind it.
They are the spiral of the samara out of the maple's longing grasp.

They are the bore of the .22 you taught us to fire, the mercy
we smell still in the rill of its blue smoke. Call them that in us

which christens the seized chambers in the heart of a Ford tractor.
Call them that which oils our own secret machinery, the quick

patter of rain's eighth notes, the run-down heels that kick up
sawdust at every dance you whirled through like the sun,

the dim lamps hung in the rafters of every unstarred night,
the lines the crow follows across the stubble-strewn fields.

Call them that which unburdens the body of its breathing,
that shuts the doors of the skull, invoking such stillness in us.

Salvation is what in us lacks grammar. But not music.
We stand in its impoverished light, calling down names

that hum in us like the rabbit's heart, unseamed by what haunts it.

*

mercy for the suicide   whose arteries   when opened to air
unleashed a storm   of crows   that devoured the quiet
mercy which left him   cloaked in black feathers

mercy that spared his mother   the slack rubble   of his body
mercy that left his heart   to sing to her
as a child does   with such hunger

mercy of the termites   and the doomed tongues
they spell   in the walls   of empty houses
mercy for the carnivorous dark   which sanctifies

erosion   mercy for the riverbank's mud   and the lapse
of dapple in its waters   mercy another name
for history   that sad anthology of frictions

*

In what key, in what sanctuary, could your voice accompany the quiet
of those who listen by holding their breath? When we stood before you,

the emptiness said everything to us. The preacher inventoried
your sins with a Pentecostal fire, and explained that he had burned up

those roads with you, carrying a can of kerosene. All that remained
to be said was said when night lit its black lamps above the heads

of the grieving. Your daughters never left your side. I saw them
young again, running to you through the rain, mirth tracing

their freckles, saying everything that was unsayable except by skin.

*

mercy for your mother's hands   gowned in flour
mercy for the angels   that danced   when she clapped
on each milled grain   mercy for each of us   giggling beneath

the soft descent   of her hand-made snow   mercy for the marrow
you had them harvest   from your bones   to save your sister
the loss you were learning   the name of   even before

it began to climb   the white rungs   of your spine

*

You would say to me that all of this is a mercy. One I have
known this entire time, even if only in the hand's small tremors.

One that bends and straightens over the field that, until now,
I left unblemished. It is here, on the last page in the book

that remains half-written, that I step down the barbed wire,
and enter the sun-struck pasture, snow and light surrendering

to my steps. And here you are, where you've always been,
where every sentence, even this one, ends with mercy.

Notes on Poems

"A Show of Hands" (page 3): The poem interpolates images from poets whose work I admire deeply—Bruce Bond, Derek Walcott, and Donald Justice.

"Tyrannosaurus Sex" (page 4): The poem's title, and some of its phrases, are from an article by Carmelo Amalfi for *Cosmos* Magazine.

"Song" (page 7): This poem is for Randall Mann.

"Sandhill Crane": (page 8) This poem is for Debora Greger.

"Of a Feather" (page 39): The poem's epigraph is from a news report by Gabrielle Bluestone originally published on *Gawker*.

"Three Hundred Byzantine Horse Skulls" (page 49): The title is a phrase in Elif Batuman's "Shipwrecks Under Istanbul," originally published in *The New Yorker*.

"Sky Valley Rider" (page 56): Charles Wright's poem by the same name is the inspiration. The end words in my poem are contained in one of his lines: "Fox fire, pale semaphore in the skull's night."

Acknowledgments

Thanks to the editors of the following publications, in which these poems, or versions of them, appear:

32 Poems	"Black Hole Factory," "Tyrannosaurus Sex"
American Literary Review	"Questions Concerning Galactic Bowling"
The Arkansas International	"The Mercy Dancers"
Birmingham Poetry Review	"The Arsonist's Lament"
Crab Orchard Review	"Song" (as "Orpheus")
Five Points	"Sandhill Crane"
Greensboro Review	"Tri-Colored Heron"
The Journal	"Sky Valley Rider," "Vertigo"
Measure	"Everyday Italian with Giada De Laurentiis"
The New Criterion	"The Shed"
Pleiades	"Mid-Century Miami," "¡Revolución!," "Step Well"
Southwest Review	"A Show of Hands"

"Story Problems" appeared in *Best New Poets 2010*, edited by Claudia Emerson and Jeb Livingood (Samovar Press, 2010).

"Tyrannosaurus Sex" was reprinted in *Old Flame: From the First Ten Years of 32 Poems*, edited by Deborah Ager, Bill Beverly, and John Poch (WordFarm Press, 2013).

"Orrery" was the runner-up for the 2017 Randall Jarrell Poetry Competition from the North Carolina Writer's Network and *storySouth*.

"Sandhill Crane" and "Homecoming" were included in *Gracious: Contemporary Poems in the 21st Century South*, edited by John Poch (Texas Tech University Press, 2018).

"Vertigo" appeared in a limited-edition chapbook from from Hayloft Press with original illustrations by Mary McManus.

I want to thank the North Carolina Arts Council, the North Carolina Writers' Network, the Sewanee Writers' Conference, the Convivio Conference, and Marshall University for awards and fellowships that supported the making of these poems.

I owe a great debt to my teachers and mentors: Thank you, Debra MacComb, Robert Whalen, Debora Greger, Michael Hofmann, David Leavitt, William Logan, Padgett Powell, Al Shoaf, Sidney Wade, Danny Anderson, Mary Jo Salter, and Vievee Francis.

Thank you to my colleagues at Marshall University. Thank you, Richard Mathews, Joshua Steward, and Sean Donnelly at the University of Tampa Press.

Thank you, friends near and far: Shannon Cole, Ben Hagen, Abi Maxwell, Jake Maxwell, Lisa Fay Coutley, Mary Beth Ferda, Daniel O'Malley, Curtis D'Costa, Lee Pinkas, Christopher Shannon, John Hart, Avani Kapadia, Allison Carey, Michael Householder, Kristen Lillvis, Joel Peckham, Rachael Peckham, Mary McManus, Blake Howell, and Ron Dupler. Thank you Austin, Alisa, Ruthie, Georgia, and Gus Hummell.

To all of my families—the Smiths, the Steeds, the Comers, the Pates, and the Sondermans—thank you.

My endless gratitude to friends and editors who found in these poems something worth saving: John Poch, George David Clark, Adam Houle, Keith Leonard, Susannah Mintz, Barbara Ras, Matthew Buckley Smith, and Adam Vines. Very special thanks to Nick McRae, Richie Hofmann, Will Schutt, Malachi Black, and Randall Mann.

Chad Davidson, Gregory Fraser, and Austin Hummell: thank you for hearing in me what I didn't know was there.

Bob and Jane Hill: this book, and I, would not exist without you.

For my best reader, and the love of my life, Laura Sonderman: thank you with all my heart for every day you have given me.

About the Author

Eric Smith was born in Carrollton, Georgia, and has lived in Michigan, Florida, and Spain. He earned his BA at the University of West Georgia, an MA from Northern Michigan University, and an MFA from the University of Florida. He was a founding editor of *cellpoems*, the innovative and award-winning poetry journal distributed via text message. He has received scholarships and fellowships from the Sewanee Writers' Conference, Convivio, and the North Carolina Arts Council. He is an assistant professor of English at Marshall University in Huntington, West Virginia, and divides his time between West Virginia and a home in North Carolina.

About the Book

Black Hole Factory is set in Adobe Jenson Pro digital fonts adapted by Robert Slimbach from the roman types cut by Nicolas Jenson in Venice about 1470, and the later italic types of Ludovico Vicentino degli Arrighi. Jenson types were the inspiration for William Morris's Golden type in the 1890s and for Bruce Rogers's early twentieth-century Centaur typeface, which is used for titling on the cover and title page. The book was designed and typeset by Richard Mathews at the University of Tampa Press.